Blue Toes

2023

First published in 2023 by Susan Glamuzina
Copyright © 2023 by Susan Glamuzina

Paperback ISBN: 978-0-473-69011-3
ePUB ISBN: 978-0-473-69012-0
Kindle ISBN: 978-0-473-6913-7
iBook ISBN: 978-0-473-69014-4

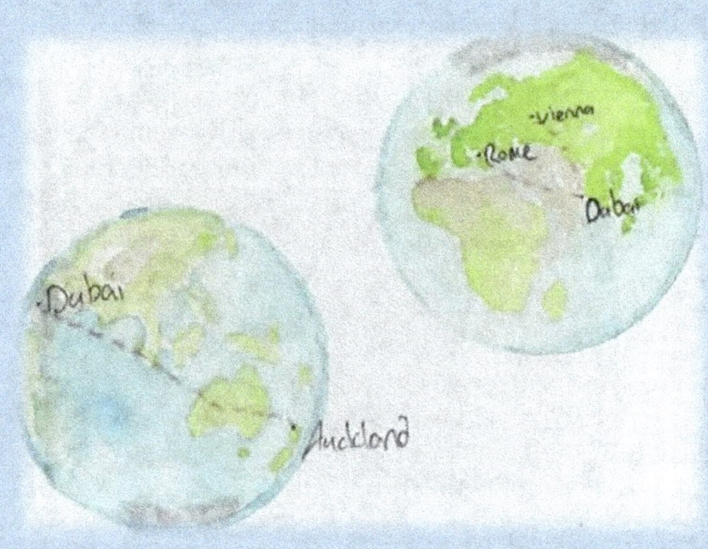

Dubai
Auckland
Vienna
Rome
Dubai

Devotion

Thanks to Lucas for being musical and all your quirky inspiration – being quirky is the best.

Thanks for making this trip so memorable to the teachers, students and parents who were on the journey with us.

Thanks to Kellie and the team at Access for your support.

Love and thanks to my Tonchi, Marco, Frankie, Val, Diana and Glen for your support so I could go on the trip.

Aroha to my creative mentors Anne Kennedy, Iona Winter and Tony McNeight, and to Bookprinting.co.nz for your support.

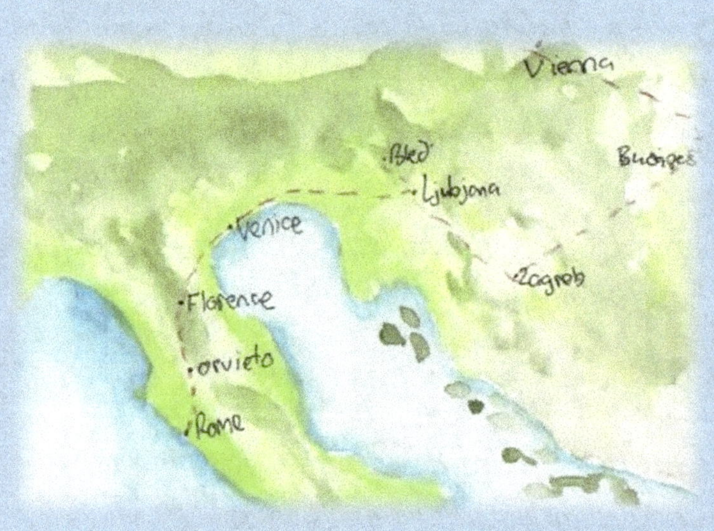

Vienna
Bled
Ljubjona
Budopes
Venice
Zagreb
Florence
orvieto
Rome

sixteen hours
constant night flight
no idea of discomfort
audio audiobook finished

creepy passenger next door
asked to sit next to my son
I smiled through my teeth
mother-hen not moving

Dubai
brightest sunrise
ever witnessed
April 4th

arrived in Italy
authentic pizza craved
fly-ridden-cafe
will wait

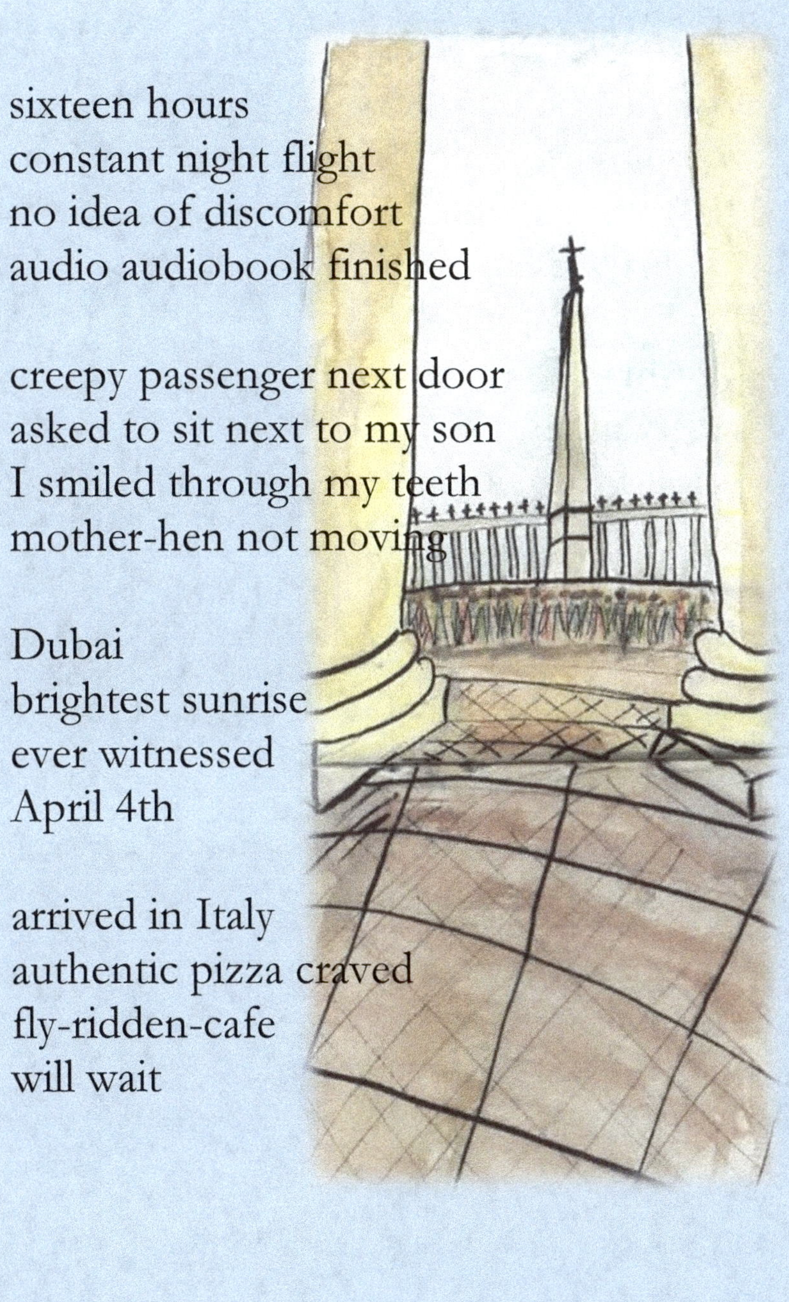

horns honking
zipping, zooming
last minute braking
Italian drivers!

mismatched rags
lost dignity
circling like seagulls
pockets got picked

gladiator's life
on the line
ten wins for his freedom
he charges into colosseum

homesick
missing my family
lost without
affection and love

early morning
tinker raindrops
flash illumination
thunder, rooster

bus becomes our home
cards, snakes and ladders
all glad to be off our feet
reminiscing and studying itinerary

Italian ambulance
sound like bag pipes
then car toy sirens
dashing to save lives

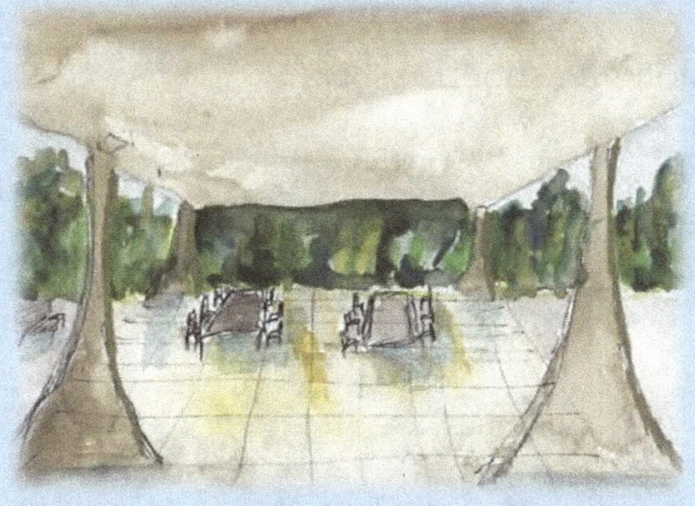

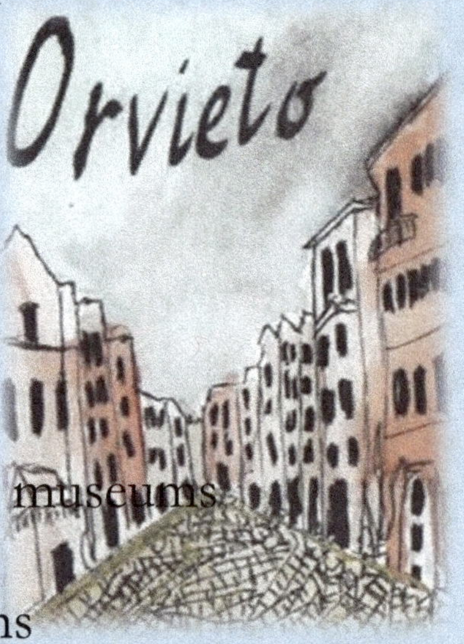

long, straight roads
vineyards and terracotta
Italian country fling past
train zips by faster

south of Florence
distant alps
icing sugar tops
breathing cool air

shops, churches, and museums
Florence rich history
money on renovations
should've gone on sewers

Bologna supermarket
self service
foreign language
constant machine beeps

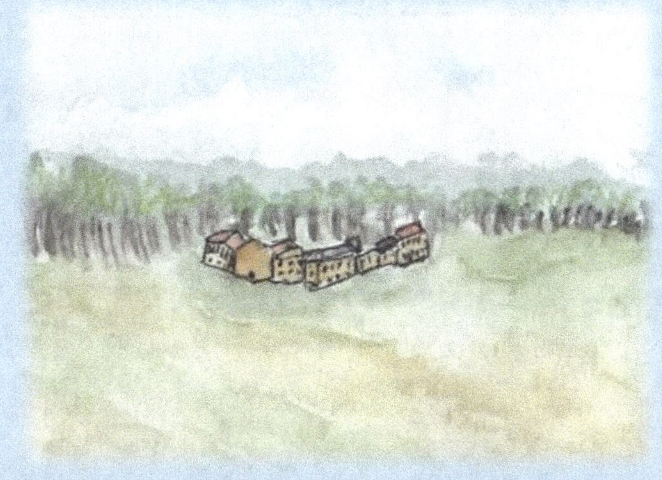

I'll never complain
about Auckland traffic again
after witnessing
Italian driving

Terracotta buildings
weeds and rubbish galore
my home streets are cleaner
Auckland appreciation

bread baskets covered in embroidered
delight
cathedral Mass in Italian
tourists photograph us we prey
Easter in San Petronius, Bologna

I asked staff for Easter Eggs
she walked me to train station
and pointed to north
instead, I bought a chocolate bar

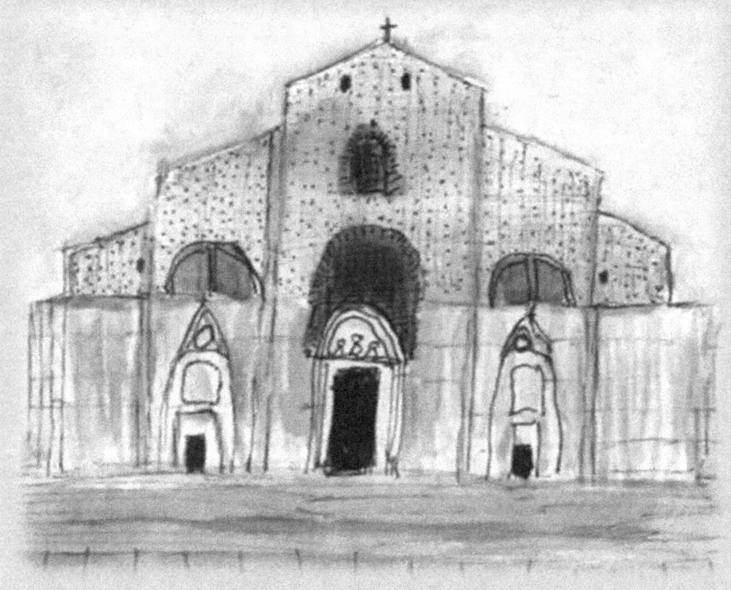

every noise echoed
through paper thin walls and floors
Bologna motel
little sleep

step, step, quicker step
to meet a walking tour
step, step, around inner cities
Rome, Orvieto, Florence, Bologna

foreign Mass
don't speak the language
still know when to stand, sit and pray
together for God

street vendor at central square
making giant bubbles for coin
if only he smiled
and lost the bubble frown

we cheated - caught the double-decker
instead of our fifth walking tour
best decision ever
rested feet, magnificent views

Piazza Carducci
The inspirational poet
from Bologna
I pen words outside his abode

they say they don't understand
English in restaurants and shops
yet they play English music
are they faking the confusion?

cathedral guarded by soldier
should I be worried of threat?
war, politic or religion?
maybe I am safer because of him

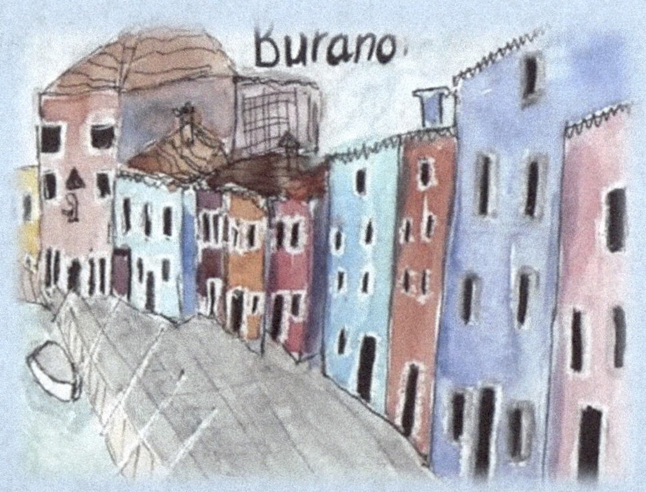

regenerated
sea-scent
beside the ocean
breathing in sea-love

glass spun on stick
red hot
ninety seconds to pull, prod and mould
he crafted a glass horse

exquisite Venice masks
depict location, statice and class
wrapped with care
prey my four don't break

Campanile of Santo Stefano
leans more every year
fingers crossed it remains strong
the Tower on Burano

multi coloured homes
canals with boats
mask, lace and glass shops
part of my heart will remain in Venice

our morning routine
rumbling wheels
pulled by yawning tourists
sixty-three suitcases

Italians celebrate
art and artists
vibrantly
long live us arties

dinner served on arrival
homey vegetable soup
my body rejoiced
Slovenia soup

brass, string, woodwind, drums
different notes in total chaos
the orchestra warms
ready to perform

bum, bum, bum, ma bum
da daa daaada daaa daa da
months, it's come together
first European concert

alps outside the window
crisp white covering the tops
can't take enough photos
scenic Slovenia

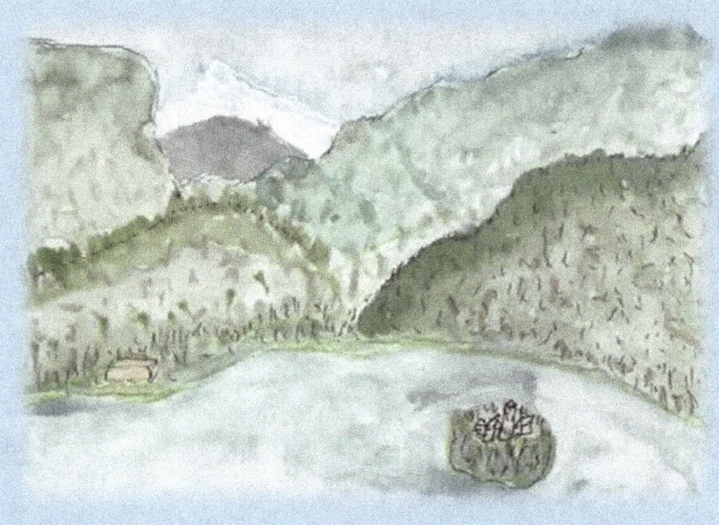

high up on the rocks
Bled Castle looks over the lake
trees and snowed alps
a scenic postcard

still water stretches
Bled Lake looks up to the castle
trees and iced alps
a scenic postcard

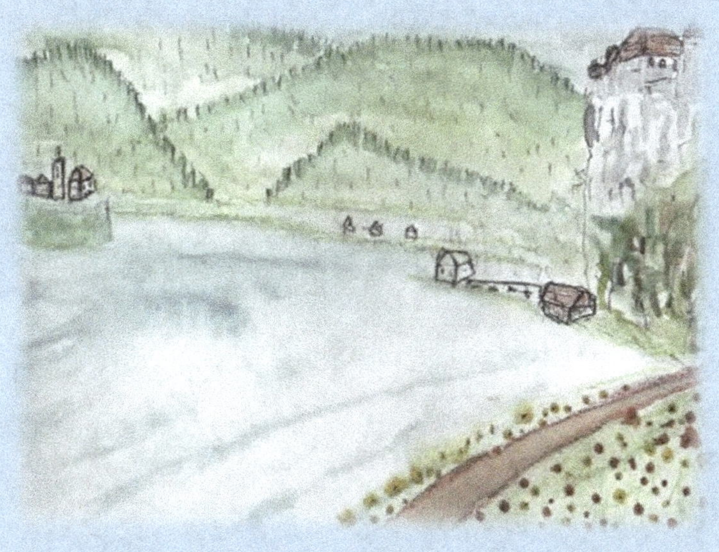

Slovenian girls clap
the kiwi boys performance
but off stage the real show begins
with a giggle

on holiday try new food
but why try
when you know what you like
cheese and ham toastie with cola

I'm from New Zealand
he, Japan. her, Italy. they, Russia
wherever born, however raised
we all smile

on a treed city square
in a rotunda
Kiwi music entertains the locals
Kongresni trg

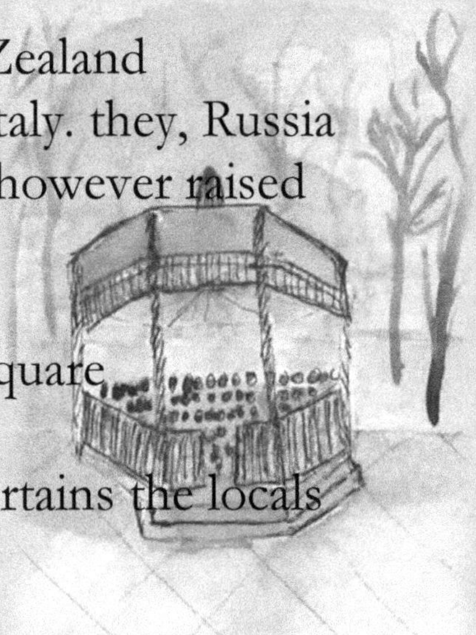

airy blue lit amenities
hidden under the town square
beside the bomb shelter
where they host concerts

video chats back home
a highlight
showing family the views
pretending we're close

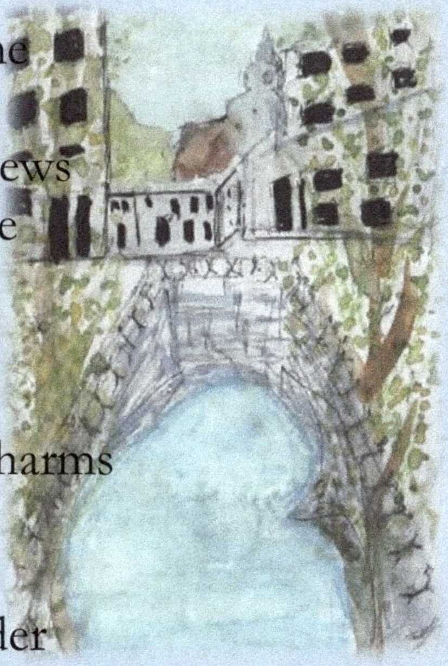

small joy for me
in a pandora bracelet
rose gold and floral charms
forever a reminder

watching for the border
to my son's cultural land
his first of many times
Dobre dosli

in shopping he came alive
his favourite tops in vibrant colours
more fun unpacking
Hrvatska footy shirts

raincoats and umbrellas
groups race between drops
followed the wrong black umbrellas
lost in Zagreb

in New Zealand
roads follow lay of land
not Europe
they just build tunnels

red and blue feet ache
need to rest but
so much to see
push through the pain

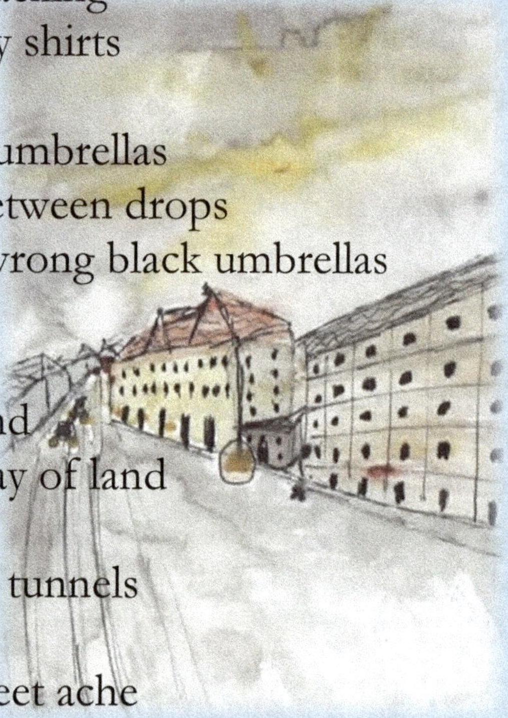

Crkva Svetog Vinka Paulskog
white and black angels sing
Croatian mass, a heavenly experience
across the world, feels like home

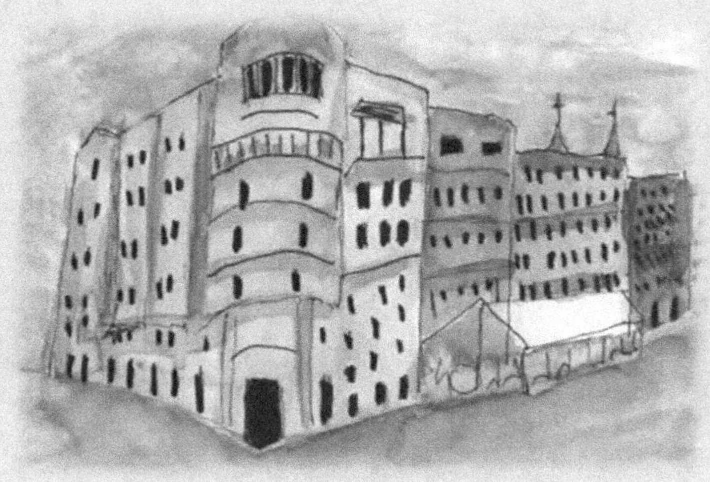

land of his forefathers
he sings in their language
dobra mali Luca
forever proud of my son

Zagreb night rain
stepping into puddles
century old paths to churches
the golden night shines

church pews are the same
beautiful yet uncomfortable
hard to sit still for an hour
torture to be in any longer

thirsty every morning
meat, bread, cheese and juice
but the juice is raro
my craving, pulp

"Second Largest Church in Budapest"
"Hottest spa in Europe"
"Third largest opera house"
everybody is so competitive

Hungary rain falls
we shuffle under umbrellas
to see horse statues
welcome to Budapest

all European Cities
churches, steps, statues
with raindrops on grey paving stones
steps, castles, more steps

Hungarian dance
traditional entertainment
a wine vase on my head
I became the entertainment

nighttime castle
cold bricks warm with glow
the long Danube river banks
shine in the dark

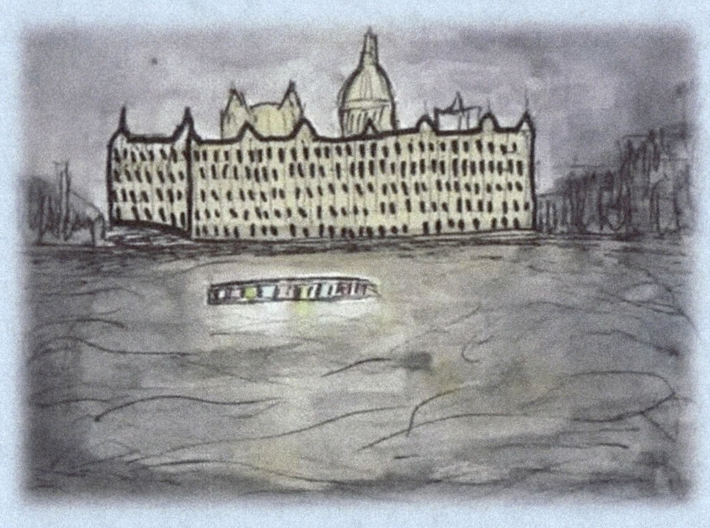

road crossings in a pack
front group take off after lights
the rest of us - lost
slow down and wait

honoured
thanks for having us
with gratitude, blessed paua cross
and manuka honey

fifty-five euros
ten-minute scenic tour in a cart
pulled by two horses
smelliest Vienna tour

paper thin walls
steps vibrate like earthquakes
at least there's a loo
hostel in Vienna

sat at a table in sweet shop
waiter sent me to counter line
counter lady said 'find seat'
Café Konditorei

surrounded by strangers
umbrellas outside St Stephen's
crying alone
need a seat, to get off my feet

clown offers to be in photos
tourists pose
his hand goes out awaiting payment
con or earning a living?

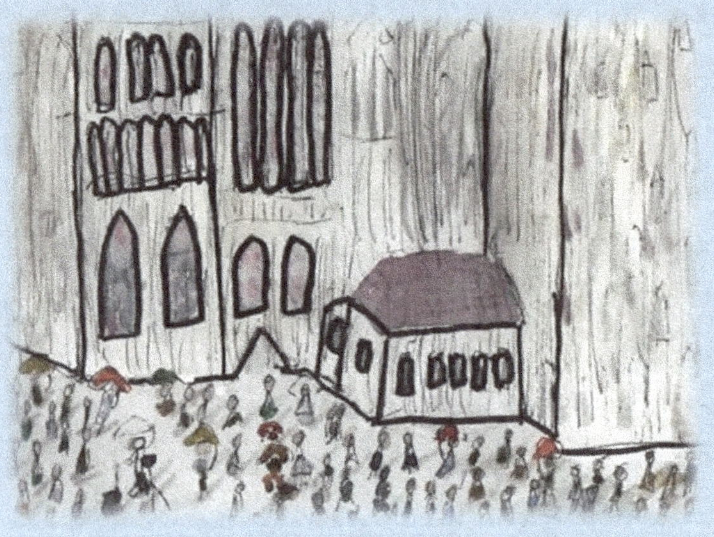

"Hallo, where are you from?"
"I'm from New Zealand."
"All is nice there."
"Yes."

are not Ozzie's
we're Kiwis
from New Zealand
no kangaroos in Austria

Italian in Rome
Croatian in Zagreb
English in Vienna
attending European Masses

pay .50 cents
swipe for the toilet
didn't work, still won't work, please
swipes, five times, busting

teacher calls out names
anxious every time
who am I rooming with?
phew – my son

my chance thirty years later
three years of learning German
in Austria, I get to speak it
but don't know any useful words

social experiment
sharing a room with other parents
intimate with strangers
I'm vulnerable

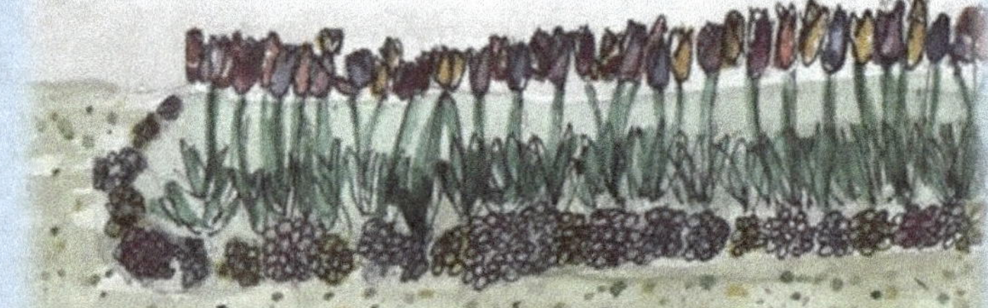

I take photos and sketch
decorated roundabouts
tulips and pansies
European spring flowers

parts of Europe shock me
smokers and dogs in restaurants
barking and puffing
great food at a cost

I don't understand tipping
waiter gets grumpy
why on me?
restaurants should pay

apartments tower over
Austrian school
slides, forts, and swings
trees, flowers, and football fields

Austrian Soup
98% water
cold spoon dips into hot liquid
with 100% flavour

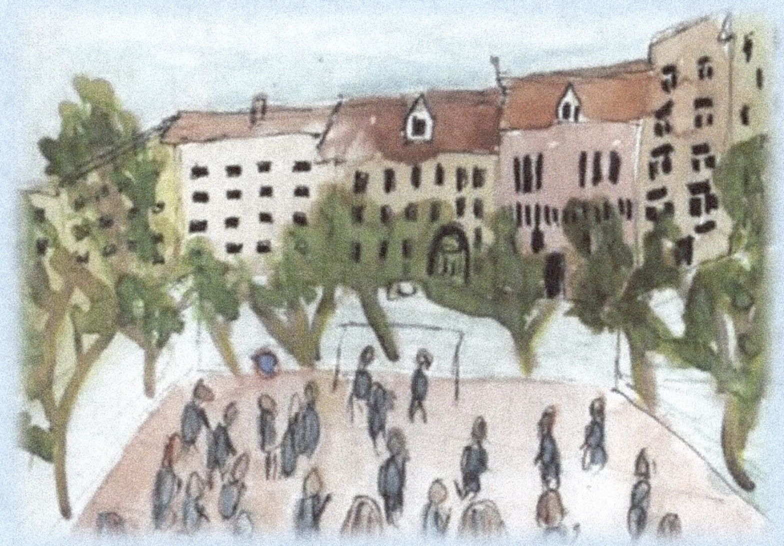

lost passport, boarded with it
where is it?
looking everywhere
found between the seats

exhausted eyes blink
red dots circle under lids
I need some sleep soon
plane seats are so uncomfortable

Dubai sky painting
sun rises
over dark storm clouds
phenomenal

tears flow on take-off
scared of handing my life away
to a pilot I don't know
relief flows at landing

happy to head home
glad to be more worldly
with sore swollen feet
board the last flight

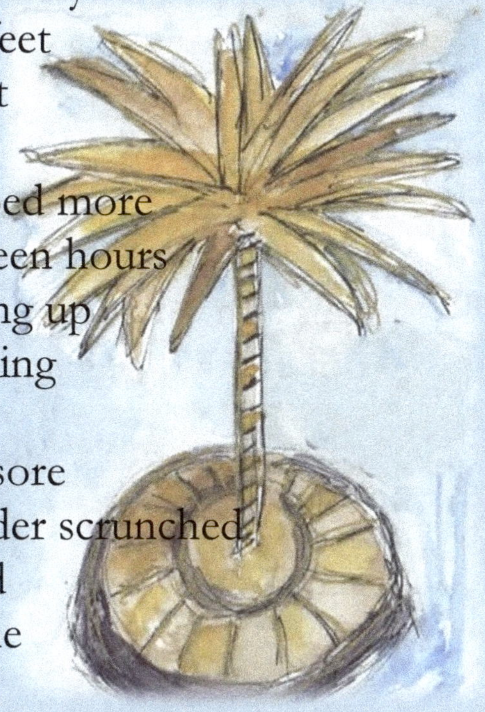

I'll appreciate my bed more
now I've spent fifteen hours
trying to sleep sitting up
dreaming of dreaming

feet swollen, back sore
nose tingles, shoulder scrunched
head dozy, eyes red
I want off this plane

fourteen hours to go
ten, nine, seven
will we ever arrive?
three, I still want off this plane

we all got blood noses
flight or air conditioning?
bloody annoying
Why?

we need more greens
not just pasta, potatoes and pizza
kids at home do too
not enough vegetables

pushed to the max
castles, churches and pizza
learnt, saw a new world
reached my limit

miss my family
pets, sleep, roast lamb, and beaches
mostly my family
and my pillow

20,000 plus
steps a day, to see churches
I need a holiday
with my feet up

my boy on the plane
sleeping on me
hurting my back, but I smile
nice to have him close

plane lullabies my son
soft music to sleep to
son changes it to AC/DC
can't sleep to Hell's Bells

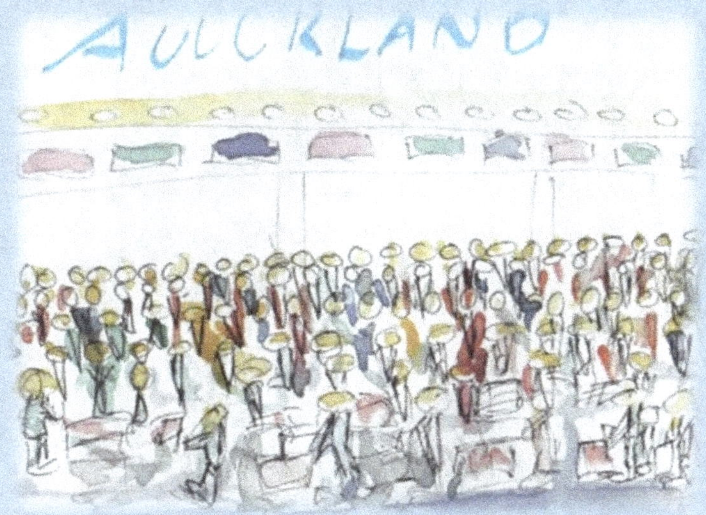

greeted the best way ever
after NZ customs
my youngest's charging hug
embracing family

sleep in my bed
holding my husband all night
bliss – not for granted
home

shattered, sleeping wrong
snoozing in day, awake at night
bugger off jet lag
oops, fell asleep during the day again

caught up on sleep
holding on to memories
back into routine
now off to print photos

Susan Glamuzina is a New Zealand author and poet who feels at home when there's sand between her toes and her thoughts are in the clouds. Susan's been published in the New Zealand Poetry Society magazine a fine line, good company lit, Spillwords, Tales of the Domain, Tales from Dominion Road, Live Encounter, and a number of international Anthology's. Susan was runner up in the national Poetry Day, Poetry at the beach and New leaf Christmas poetry competition2022. NZ National Poetry day 2023 featured in Titirangi village window, short listed in the poets XYZ's Childrens Poetry competition.

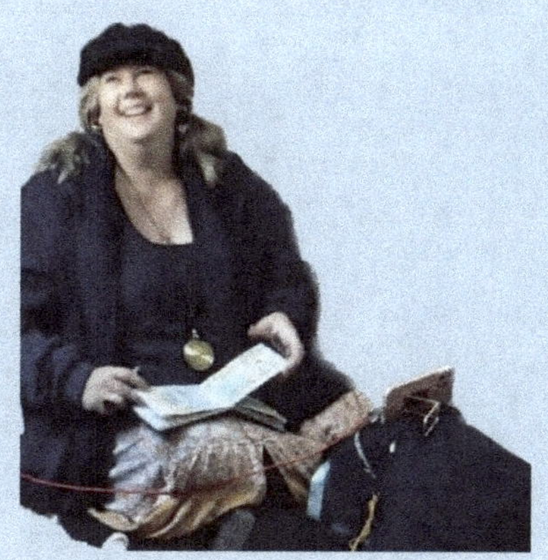